Naming the Beasts

Naming the Beasts

Elizabeth Morton

OTAGO UNIVERSITY PRESS
Te Whare Tā o Te Wānanga o Ōtākou

Contents

Feral

Everything wild in you is held in pockets. You watch the webcam like a fish.
I want to hear you bark the milk truck up its cul-de-sac. I want to arrange flowers
in the shape of a feral thing. I want to find you in the thick of the lake,
or in the tributaries that bleed out black, the soot and shine of star systems
more far away than the first hearth to illuminate this sad valley.
We are a small sound, you and me. We eat boiled corn and jerk chicken
as if we were people, as if we knew electric toasters and underwater cables
and recognised combat only by its economy. You could have been a warrior,
before you were this cotton heartbeat – this hush of sparrows.
If you were a dancehall, you would be flooded. The bandstand and the furniture
and the banjos bobbing soft as paperwork. What are you
but an evacuated party, people gathered in the stairwell with their napkins
and cigarettes wondering whether this is just a drill. *Is this just a drill?*
Have you forgotten why you came, from the woods and into the village?
Have you forgotten the rhino scat, and wild dogs giggling – how night
stalks even the flimsiest postures? Remember the ponies in the moonfields,
buckling under geese that have the audacity to cut the sky in halves?
You hold your words, softly. You are a smudge of beast,
a grey track cut into the evening. You leave the party, carrying only heat.

Grief

The hickory tree is dying outside the window.
It dies slow and shy, like grass blanched beneath a copper.
The copper drowns the grass like a metaphor.
You can drown in six centimetres of water.
Sometimes you wake to a realisation
you were drowning all along. The hickory tree
is not drowning, but is a metaphor for ache.
Five stages in, white as a summer ocean, Kübler-Ross
opens the window, like the window
is a metaphor for reductionism, like reductionism
is just a fancy name for a bunker, dug into the vertebra
of clay. We are all dying. Even Kübler-Ross kicked a bucket
sometime we can find on Wikipedia.
The hickory tree is dying, and the window is a prayer we say,
as the doorbell bleats and a girl with a scythe
comes to sell shares in repurposed carpet.
The window is a metaphor for everything we expect
and everything that falls short. The hickory tree
dies with its head in its hands. The window is a pain
we cannot touch.

Linnaeus eats the ocean

In the first instance, he names the bivalves after genitalia.
With a speculum, he registers each for their architecture –
hatch and staircase, shaft and manway. Listen.
A pipi is a woman, squinting through a shut door.
A cockle is a woman who buys her own drink and holds it
like a treaty. An oyster has a butter knife in her jacket pocket
and opens other things, but never takes off her hat.
Quiet! This is a world where a joke is a wave that curls
like a lie, folds in on itself. I have a fear of oceans,
the grip and the slow-motion of them. Swells that sway buoys
under the lullaby of moon. Moons that sway oceans
like women. Women whose bodies are smudged pastels,
mauve and krill-pink, the muted tongues of things that know
frailty is not feebleness. Silence. The water holds
its properties like they conjure the beast itself.
The algific households of deep-sea shelves are songless
and blind. There is no language to coruscate a love.
The salt of a joke about clams sticks to his hands,
in the thick of cul-de-sacs and grocery stores.
In dreams, the things he names manifest on a platter,
erubescent and full frontal. The tide wipes the spittle
and the foam crust from its chin, while he unpicks
the ocean with a butter knife. Open open.

Old doggo barks the world

Old doggo is hugged by the parentheses of dusk, one bracket narrowing in on another.
The moon trades a pencil for a cigarette. The stars stand like catchers in the outfield,
dodging space junk and satellites, watching each other's waiting,
like waiting is the real sport. Old doggo sniffs out night-cats in the bramble and gorse-wire.
He moves like rain on a metal roof, all paws and staccato hammerings. Dusk,
and the slur of birds who hoot sundown doom. Old doggo sniffs the mosquito doors
of people with barricades against wild that visits like a knick-knack salesman,
all Tupperwares and handshakes. City folk chew confectionary in their sitting-rooms,
fend off nothing and the albumin of moon. Old doggo pisses on mailboxes,
rosemary, the slim trunks of guava trees. If he were a real dog,
he would upturn the mattresses, stir people from the delta waves of sleep,
open midnight refrigerators and drag out chickens and cantaloupe.
He would trot in and out of avenues, barking the headlines of other galaxies,
woof woofing the trajectories of asteroids as they slip the membrane of earth's old eyeball.
Old doggo would *woof woof* the violet drifting, *woof woof* the known universe
cupped by scare quotes like the whole thing is ironic. Old doggo would be chased by boys,
into the bowels of infrastructure, for his slander of something so big
that irony is blasphemous. They would throw cartoon grenades,
and old doggo would yap and die, again and again.
He would lower himself into the canyon of a conurbation that moves in and out of itself
like a river. He would bury his tongue in blue glitter. He would eat the shadows
of a god who operates by stealth, but can't disguise his gamy scent.
Old doggo would rise with the dawn chorus of forklifts and derricks
and slink back to a carpeted tenement, a rectitude of command and compliance,
the slight solace of an ottoman and a possum hide, the parentheses of upholstery.

Mower

The dumb patience of grasses, gossip of eucalyptus purple-backed
and chittering. Ancient washcloth of oil and blood and the lullaby
of primer, carburettor, my father's lungs that clench and unclench.
An ox heart is a jackfruit quenched with heat and horror. My father
peels back honeysuckle from the soft brains of hydrangea.
He coaxes asparagus weed from the mouths of burrows,
while his wireless spits words without a catcher – scratched choir
of men who hold morals like munition. My father on the pullcord
cancels the callers, dismantles the cicadas that crackle and fizz
on a day urgent with sky. The rusted chassis grunts, and it is this way
as it has always been. The same motion of a chief and herdsman,
the cut engines of our infancy, green acres aching with birds.

Driving north

Every day we drive past the dead ox. A satchel of blowflies,
sticky aquarium, a marmalade where jelly and pith cling
to the shrunken sockets of bone. A month ago, the beast bellowed
vowels across the daisies, looked to the mountains for a calm
that called him north like a compass. We moved here from a rut
of factories and stoplights. Allergic to the infrastructure of things
with gas pipes and garages and fish markets and train yards,
buildings that ooze into the green hillocks and scudded skies,
we sucked inhalers and drank calamine. Now, we drive past
the ox like he is a landmark, a signpost to a country
where even dead things pulse and rattle. We wind down
our windows to smell a crime of passion, a funk of cells
destroying cells. Autolysis is what we did in the suburbs,
chewing at our own rind and waving at neighbours all the while.
Over infomercials with TV dinners, calculating our lives
in episodes and seasons, until meaning was bone dry and spent.
Like us, the ox knew his doom inside out, the inevitability
of tics and maggots working through him like time.
We moved north to unpick the stars from a rash of city lights.
We followed mountains that dolphin through a clot of black,
and listen to oxen warming up for prayers we can't translate.
When he kneeled down to die, the mountains called to him,
motherly and mewing. Now wasps reanimate the chant.

Stalker

What if I am a tree falling in a forest and nobody hears?

What I would give to heal   the dull   thud   of a kitchen light,
to touch the filament, gently   and wet. I stand at night-time hedges
building worlds   in other people's yards. A technician of   lives
that pass gently   as   mosquitoes, taking little parts of   my kith
and holding them   in lukewarm bellies.   Spreading love
like the   third-world disease it is.   I want you to know I take
batteries and batteries. My torch   forces   itself into a future
cryptic and dark like   these poems.   Your dogs bleat –
two brontosauruses, big and dumb, and I have inherited them.
I have inherited the bicycles in the carport, your television shows,
the way you leave your teabag on the saucer. When I   deliver
your newspaper, I want you to   look for   me –
in the connections columns or in the   deaths. The kitchen light
is a lonely thing. I hope somebody is looking in   from the hedge
from the   biblical crosshairs   or from behind a tree in a forest
where the trunks are ringbarked   or someplace   else.

Listen.

What if my brain is in a vat, and I don't know?

Cogito ergo   something. I am   a brain in the chlorinated pool,
sun webbing   the surfaces. I am   meat cannibalising   other meat.
Do you know I loved you   once – loved you by your   numberplate,
by the cul-de-sac   that ends with your   front door.   Hell,
        I remember walking past you in the supermarket. Your mouth-hollow,
your shellac-fingertips, your gym gear worn with   premeditated indifference.

Did you see me? I was   there. A warm organ steeping in a summer
full of curtains. You were   there. That was the summer the sinkhole
sank the carpark. People with parcels of ham hocks and squash,
clucking like poultry. I   watched   them watch. I was glad for complicity,
the snugness of   proximity. The cockles of my cortices were bathwater-warm.
I was a blue hill in the background of a scene about   happiness.
I like to think my inputs and outputs register on the machine. Grid paper
that charts sentiment, up and up.   What   am I,
but a bain-marie of leftovers. Love is something to swill a little,
to expectorate   into a spittoon.   What   am I, but the tannins
that catch in your throat.   Whatever.   You were there. I see you.

Trolley problems

Would I save Syria or my dog?   My sister or the trade towers?
          Flight 370 or my dignity?   If the train is heading for Mengele, tied to the tracks,
would I re-route it?   If six children are on one course   and you are on the other
          how will I know if you love me as much as I love you?
Thought experiments make villains of us all. I'll never be on a desert island with just one
1980s anthem. I'll never have to choose between my parents and my country – just between
Advanced Whitening or Maxi White or Enamel Pro or Ultra Cavity Protection.
          Death is a loser   who watches *Judge Judy* and reheats sweet and sour chicken.
Death drinks Red Bull and does Sudoku,   and I can see something of
myself there – unsolicited house calls and standing by night-time hedges,
looking in.   You see, I want to die in the daisy constellations of your front yard,
like the mawkish   romantic I am. I want to ride my   BMX
past the swing set to your porch, and I want you to ring the police
and peg me down with your two kind hands.   That is what   love is.
          I would re-route the nexus of causality and time,   for you.

I would send trains smashing through a Rube Goldberg machine,
one domino
falling another, because that's what love is   too.
Hell, I want to hold the kitchen light by the filament,   gently and wet,
        to conduct heat and have it pass through me. And hope somebody
will pay witness,   maybe.

Kuroko

They could hear me coming – down the birch,

crashing into scrub like something that lands, indemnified.

I am the acrobat who did not mean to break the fall net.

What rib do you come from? They ask that sometimes.

I was bone and bristle and six. I was down the birch,

into the house. And then opening wrong drawers,

pulling steak knives where I wanted for sponge.

What rib do you come from? And it was just my luck

to trace the crumbs back to the witch,

to gun the axeman down in a clearing of wood.

They could hear me on my way – before I crossed the centre line,

before I held the twitching universe like a pup.

I am a story where the house is made of sponge cake,

and the liquorice caryatids hold the guttering

like it's the right thing to do. I am the witch in the oven –

the coda that never gave you the juicy details

but ended in kids walking down a watercolour driveway,

met by dogs and potted begonias. *What rib?*

I am the things that make the other things true.

In my latest dream, I am a kuroko who furls a scene

before the players speak the script. *What …*

I muffle my body. I dress in black. I dream of descent.

Birdlife in a broken century

I

I'm a delinquent, skipping the stony tenements
that belch smoke and invective. I leap TV aerials,
scuttle slow as thunder along the window ledges
ducking chickhood 'mares and cigarette ash tapped
from the bedrooms above. I'm a buzzard,
inconspicuous and dull-eyed. I'm a lifetime of birds.
I've been tarred and feathered like a snitch
and left for dead in the village stocks. Apples, stones –
the shrugged sadism of people who swat spiders,
whose barn animals know them by a blur of timber.
I could run into the fauna of gentler suburbs.
I could talk to the bobby calves waiting in the trailers,
moo soft milk vowels and hope the blood of one
does not rattle the breath of its brother. I am guilty
of queuing, shamefaced at the altar, begging for meat.
Forgive me; forgive my hands their collateral.
If I am the birds, I know just what I take.
If I am the sky, I hold the buzzards like my heart.
If I am a person, there can only be attrition and slick sawdust
between this thing and the next.

II

Everything I touch is flames. I knit heat to its animal.
I'm the drought of the leap year, the marrow lapping
in the dry bone. I could eat my own rind, lick the salt
from the edges of me, but I would not be sated.
At the altar, I fetch exoneration like a stick.

Here is the skillet and here is the heartbeat;
here is the iron and the winter and the hangover
that comes upon waking in a supermarket aisle
where no beasts bray. In the next life I am plastic –
tonnes and tonnes of clingfilm and polystyrene beans.
Look, the mattress is on fire! Look, I'm on my tiptoes,
yet the ocean is over my head! If I had a dollar
for every time I strike a match, I'd be a rich man.
As it happens, everyone I know is a pyromaniac.

III

Ma said leave only footprints. My carbon footprint
is a kilometre across and six miles deep.
Last week I made a nest with bubble wrap and hair
for all the kids I'll never have.
At the altar they say I'm a Zero but they do not see
the scope of my despair.
If I am a bird I am stuck circling the carnage.
If I am a person I'm sat in a burning car listening to radio songs
and dialling numbers of friends I don't see in real life;
not even the jaws of life will find me.

Rabbits

Where we shot rabbits at dusk, our rifles sticky with remorse.
The bullets dissolved into a world of broth and stew, of rabbits repurposed
and ready for a tablescape of crockery and soup ladles
and talk about fiscal policy and the backlog of grievances
conceded by people without ancestors. We stand on shoulders.
Ghost bodies floating through land so vital it burns. Green assault,
an agony of hills tumbling through hot skies.
Where we shot the rabbits, we hung them from the rafters,
blunt bodies shedding burrow-lust and foot-thud.
There is a gap between one deception and another,
a circuitry of hope. The rabbits have no inkling of what is lost.
The grass the grass the grass and the under-grass, all open
to a predatory god whose paws are dumb and everywhere.
Dusk, we shot the rabbits, and couldn't stomach our own conquests.
All open and without history, the grass the grass.

We write what we know when we run out of things that we don't

In somebody else's poem I hold the rotary phone to my head like a gun.
I dial ones like they own the place. I want to go to a semi-detached flat
in a heaven where the septic tanks don't overflow. In somebody else's poem
I'm a felled tree, oscillating with woodlice. They would have me kneeling
by the gate, or lying foetal in a city square. The lice would take me slow
and warm. In somebody else's poem I'm eating fried chicken wings
in front of Judge Judy. I'm chewing the bones like a dog, deciding whether
Judge Judy's hair is better now than it ever was in the '90s.
In somebody else's poem it's goddamned desolate. I'm in a house
with no windows; just venetian blinds on blank walls. The rotary phone
bleats hircine, and I hold a real gun to my head. In a poem, the gun goes off.
I wake in another poem, planting succulents because love goes as far
as my toes, and no further. My uncle who never writes might write a poem
where we drive to Karangahape Road and egg people who wear tinsel.
In that poem I am smaller and my arms won't work. I can't stop throwing
egg after egg, and they coagulate on the overpass tarseal.
In somebody else's poem I'm eating meat. I look the beast in the eyeball
and moo. My friend, who is no longer my friend, might have me moo
along Karangahape Road, wearing tinsel. Somebody will hit me with an egg.
I will be the cow, in somebody's poem. In another, I will be the gun.

Maps

The passage of a forage-blower, slow and certain.
Heavy smell of sun and chaff, gold passing through the metal gums.
We live in a spatter of locusts. Bleached blonde and dry, scar tissue
where the political map cuts conterminous fields for attention.
Even the crows recognise the edges of things, eggshell configurations
that hold their fringes like a knife. Flat acreages that pulse
under the summer. Soils that shudder with the touch of a hand-fork,
that wince with the plough mule's hoof-fall. This world is a fragile flower.
It acts out, under the cold vigil of moons and midges. It bites its tongue,
and waits in an Accident and Emergency ward, wringing love
from the nurse whose gestures are clinical. This world is degenerate.
Its fields are salt-drenched, crops are brittle
and skinny as dogs. Cartography is a four-point restraint,
a temporary hold, guarding ipseity of things without names,
of flora and fauna dysregulated and dim as words
in other people's languages. This land is a diva,
putting on a good show. A disinhibition of shadow and noontime
crickets, and the scat of effluence drying on the creekbanks.
There is a break between one state and the next. Still,
the forage-blower moves like time –
a metronome, quiet comfort to a scape burned-out and bitter.
The crows tippytoe around the edges. Blisters wax and wane.

If we are alone

Something is the eye of the storm, the distance between dreams.
Like a fly in a cathedral, like radishes on a quarter acre, the sour jellies
of a mouse on the airport tarmac. Our star is an average star.
We are average people, hashing out a harvest in the yellow hill-country.
Something is the riddle between one surface and another.
Our pith, our dark casings, hold us back. We are small and ungrateful,
not by plan but by programme. We inherit the routines of our gods.
Our sleepy ceremonies carry us in diminishing circles. We stall
at signs and read them for a fate we cannot bend.
If there is extra-terrestrial life, they reply in the language of television.
They will congregate in shopping malls and colossal cinemas,
eating food-court curry and joking about average people
in average cul-de-sacs, emptying WasteMasters and upchucking
cheerios in ordinary toilets. Something is the gap between sentience
and sentiment. Something is a pea compared with a beachball,
and a beachball compared with the Atlantic. If we are alone,
we are seedheads bursting with a million little timetables.
By the end, we'll have the paperwork in order.
We will meet our maker from a distance of two metres, with PPE
and a hazmat suit. In between dreams – that is nothing at all.

Castles

We fetch the cutlery of battle, and shelter in the pīngao sedge,
our   silly   hearts rinsing themselves in fear-juice.
What miniscule violations of the unwalled country?
Sand and saltwash,   as needful as a wrecking ball
sucking its teeth while we watch the steeple undo itself.
The slip of a hardwood twig, the tide a   gag reflex.
Jimmy's watchtower slumps. Meredith's cat's-eyes
leave the kingdom and return,   leave and   return.
We would find Jimmy's backpack at Castlepoint,
sometime after   1989. The marram grass and lupin
would tell us nothing of the heart.   I wouldn't know
what happened to Meredith, I think she   might work in event management
and watch the news   the way a guard watches   a convict
the way autumn watches   the sky weaken and fall.
1989   and the cordons were mounted,   our lives cut
and pasted into a storyboard   none of the players
recognise.   I RSVP'd to the event and didn't show up
but the tide leaves   and returns   and leaves.

Instructions on how to lose a mind

First, bark the moon. Make ceremony from a stammer,
from a steaming crockpot of two-minute noodles,
from the way the taxi driver sucks his bottom teeth as he drives you north.
Hold the flame of truth in a wastebasket. Carry it from room to room,
making little psalms about a horizon as unsteady as a Sunday drunk.
Burn down a kitchen. Watch the Honey Puffs and Coco Pops go up, like silver trees.
Watch eggs pop and ooze, punctuation for the heartburn of a mammal
who sees hope in erasure. Be the subtraction. Be an anorak in a kingdom of orange.
An umbrella that feathers into a soft polymer rain. This is heat.
This is the truth disguised as someone bolder. Don't tell yourself this is real
or that you live at the checkpoint between one ontology and another.
They say an arsonist will stand on a hillock to watch the sun touch down
over an ecosystem of fuel. To lose a mind, be that fuel.
The sun will make a fire-starter of you yet. But this is an instruction.
To lose a mind, register the fraudulence of seasons. Hold autumn to account.
Walk circles around spring like it is a sick kitten. Flowers
are a sign of abandoned hope. The stems of an iris, bruise-necked and soft.
To lose a mind, swallow mountains. Swallow risperidone, clozapine, olanzapine.
Hold your breath until you purple and bend. View an eclipse from a dayroom
window where the glass is unshatterable. Be an unreliable narrator.
Adjust truth by its pullcord. Confabulate stories of hunt and haunted.
Truth is a flame that shapeshifts, that interrogates the gyri of credulous brain.
Were you there, after all? To lose a mind, ask this every day.
Live like you're on fire. Live like you're on fire and running.

Burn night

The field is a crouch of trees. Fire and fir, and a balsawood plane
that cuts lice from the night's black pelt. A mynah lifts a snail,
and strikes against the cattle grid. Is it instinct or tradition – this sober
murder, this beak keeping time like we could never? What good
will come of us, jesters around a flame, chewing peppermint and detangling
our fathers' faces from our mothers'? Fire and remembering.
A snail is hammered from its shell. The plane falls somewhere
between the troughs and the cricket pitch. We will find it on the other side
of loss. We will come to it on the day the chicks leave the heat lamp,
the day you take the truck to the city to buy Lucky Strikes
because you know the agony of permission, the smell of beeswax
when it hits 63 Celsius and makes the sky steeper. Night.
The mynah carries the snail to the dog stars, drops it on a traffic island
someplace it wouldn't make a difference. What difference
does it make, all these nights trying to burn the world into us?
Little orange globe of your Lucky Strike – and it is all I carry.
A madeleine of smoke on smoke.

Eternal recurrence

Jupiter is my happy place. I am never there. Born again and again
to the same flat – surfacing to a kitchen countertop with a cantaloupe,
a washing machine stomping something Russian.
I have been falling in love with lies people tell. I have been catching my soul
in the hall mirror, and it's haunted as heck. I have been buying my fables.
There's me in the woodlands, a wolf in a red coat. There's me
purchasing four-bean mix at the self-checkout, plotting an out.
There's me tromping the pavements, thwarted by the supermassive
black hole at the centre of my fever dream. I hold my self like ice.
I watch *Dr. Phil* because Tolstoy said you shouldn't turn away.
A woman drinking hand sanitiser. A woman shoplifting Tic Tacs
in a Walmart store. A woman born again and again to a sex cult.
Don't get me wrong. I'm happy enough. I'm kidding
when I say I'm buying four-bean mix and air-drowning while Pam
from aisle seven massages my heart to see if it's still there.
Jupiter is my happy place. I was never a fable wolf in a red coat.
I lie down, a coward's prevarication. I catch my soul
in the bus shelter glass and it's just other people blinking back.

Poem in which we sleep at the wheel

Night is not adenosine   catching in your cortices, delta waves
     rolling slow and long over black silt. Night is a heron hosting a landfill –
glitter-lit and stench and sentiment of past lives, of mangoes left too long,
     a Britney doll from   2007, a postcard of two towers. Night is a joke
told by a news anchor, about moonwalking and children too young to say   yes,
     or Laika, barking sad vowels from orbit. Night offers no remuneration.
Night is where I hold you down and wake up. Or where you hold me down
     and   you wake up, and I was just a   figment. At best I was a dream
about the way serious things all become punchlines with time. With time
     sleep looks like wakefulness, and you've been sleeping all this while,
and the spindles look the same. You sleep through daytime soaps,
     intimacies, drives to the park swings, and find yourself ordering CC & drys
at a grungy bar where life has taken you, meek and earnest,
     like it was   the easiest thing.   Night chases us into the corners
where I hold my hands up like guns. Where the guns turn into owls.
     Where I hold up two things that burn into my fingerprints,
like time might have done
     anyhow, if I'd given it long enough.

The lost ones

We are lost, in our luffing raincoats, bent at the wharf edge,
windward chatter spitting birds across the seascape. Our sky,
long and bruised. Bargemaster and wharfinger reading the wounds
of bar and trough, feint gale, roll and chop, slop and slam of green
on green. We are lost on meadows and farms, the glassy anchor
of an afternoon. The sun, a paperweight, and all the yellow rays.
Milkwitch and conker, land-dry and salt-burned,
we are small barometers of a weather that comes milky as a dream.
We are lost to the almanac of kinfolk. We are words that curdle
at the gloaming, that resist the blunt light of a spell about hard things.
We are soft mammals, digging our friends into coral banks,
holding their wrist bones to our ears to hear the sadness of the sea.
We are the honeyfur and pollens smudged on their shirtsleeves,
lichen and parasite entering a space where words become wolves
carrying their pups by their lily-stems. We are captains of cloud,
heavy and haunted. We slip down the throats of people agape
with the wonder of this elaborate trickery. Soft and soft,
we see the shadow and we enter.

A history of wading backwards

The mangroves burn like effigies.
The moon is so black, these days. They can't say when it turned.
The estuary that flanks the motorway is home to a savage magic
that cursed you a mermaid with scales that chatter like rain.
We get legless on sangria and our tongues sit hot and heavy
in our mouths. There is no comeback from ascent.
We were young once. We knew how to hold things.
I had a friendship bracelet with five different girls.
I don't know if you kept your half of the bargain. You were taller
and you had a favourite Spice Girl and I didn't know any tunes
except for something by Kenny Rogers about somebody so beautiful
and I wanted to be Kenny more than even Baby Spice. I wanted a smoked-out
voice and a guitar. I wanted to serenade beautiful things
from the bottom of a fire escape. Things that glitter with ruin.
You were a mermaid in the '90s, the same way I was a meltdown.
You ate paninis and spirulina from mall cafés, tucking your tail
under the vinyl stools. You drank from public fountains,
and did the MJ moonwalk that I could never do.
We used to swim, in that pool with the pea-green
ceiling tiles, with the vending machine that only issued K Bars.
Old women would undress in the changing rooms
and we would renounce all bosom and girth and puberty.
You would wag your tail fins and I would sing low and smoky,
and the old ladies would unpick their bathing suits and talc up,
and we would never get to twenty-five, we'd swear bluely.
Twenty-five was all dressed up with nowhere to go.
We planned to doggy-paddle until our gills caved in
and our limbs wrinkled up like sultanas. You were a swimmer
and I was a punchline. A stone in a poet's pocket.

We were swimming when Princess Diana stopped breathing
and we were swimming when our character-crush from *My Girl*
was taken by a swarm of bees. There are signs on the way there.
We waded into the estuary, moon-black and ready.
We swam until you were a mermaid and I was someone falling.
Only some of us come back.

Metaphors are for pussies

1.

I want to say it real. The rupture of another day wringing hands
and wiping blood from the neck of the hen. I'll talk wolf.
I'll say language stalks the best poultry, and arranges them, tail up
along the porch rail. I want to not speak in metaphor. There is no hen.
I did not rupture another vessel. I am wolf, if only because I'm not fit
to be anyone else. I dog-ear pamphlets about the way metaphor
is a pathology and there is a medicine. The chairs are laminate.
If they catch me, it'll be the moment I reach for a Kleenex. Is that real?
That is real. The doctor says I didn't kill the hen. Wolf, I say.
I want to say it real. But if they want to catch me, I will run for the hills.

2.

This is better. This is more real than the last one. The pamphlets
have a photograph of somebody like me but more so.
I am in a coop, with creatures who smell and howl like I do.
Sometimes we eat chicken wings, and it is uncanny
that we can register ourselves in mirrors. Still. Language is a spade
I lean on, the same spade that splits the neck of the hen.
Blubbery syllables spatter out like relief. Is that how it feels?
I have been sick so many years, and if that's how it feels—
But I am a feral thing, without the dignity height affords.
I feel like this is becoming unreal again. The feathers glitch out.

3.

I want this to be the best one. The one with the realist thing out.
Picture this: I'm in a clearing, surrounded by people who love me
if I do what they say. Sometimes I do what they say. I take from the woodland
inkberries and deference. I wear my wolf onesie and piss on other things.
I'm in a clearing looking up. It hurts more that way, staring space
dead in the eye, grappling with the god who's on call, or who has buggered
off for the weekend. I try to not be an angry person. I nose breathe
and make origami with the tightest folds. I want to be the best one.
I'm in a clearing and people who love me hand me a hen to break.
It's easy-peasy, they say, it's a fucking walk in the park.

4.

It's my blood, not the hen's. I'm as real as the rupture of day.
I'm the one with the height and the howl that makes me a loved person.
The brochure says this is a metaphor involving diabetes.
This is nothing like diabetes. I am not an angry person if I can help it.
The nurse moves like a dancer. She is the sort of person I could be,
if I had no shred of myself. It's easy-peasy, they say. A fucking walk in
the park, high as a fucking kite on fucking drugs I can't pronounce.
I'm the type of person to fold my origami tight. I fold the neck
in on itself, like it's natural to live in the brace position. A cinch.
I make friends in the brace position. I'm a wolf, but they won't know.

5.

The hens could not stomach me from the get-go. I did circles
in a clearing, before I had the nouns to make vegetation a real thing.
This is another most real thing. I walked the corridors with a brochure
about the symptoms and prognosis of existential dread. I did circles.
The hens caught in my throat. I wanted them to love me
with the same energy I hated myself. Take that! Language is a spade
I lean on. That is not a metaphor. No. The chairs are laminate.
I trace the real people with my hands. What is this?
It's a walk in the fucking park – that's what. It's me
throwing poultry-feed at the moon, like it's something else.

Widdershins

Wolf rhymes with nothing, holds the giddiness of galaxies
by the scruff of their necks. A whirl counter-clockwise,
and flung into a meadow of oxalis. I have gone to seed,
spent on love and the hot breath of cosmic background radiation.
Under a sun that opens chatoyant and heavy over the farm,
the wafture of poplars that have forgotten how to shed.
Winterless, we enunciate our names like they will hold
years from now, like the meadow might breathe us into permanence.
Wolf rhymes with nothing, but stalks the green like he owns the place.
His own wingman, a grey blur of hammering purpose.
The oxalis sweeps like cilia. The ground-birds tessellate and scatter.
If Wolf could peg one down, he would. It is all an animal can do.
The lily neck of something victim, the theatre of first degree.
Sometimes I am unlikeable and old and head-drunk.
I look to Wolf for an opening, a sure-footed prologue to beast and blood.
Andromeda breathes down my neck, and I can visualise a world
hurled upon an other world, without invitation. I am prey, mostly,
a buckling wildebeest, propitiating the hunger of sharper figures.
Wolf is what the hours bring. Meekness turned outmoded and dogged,
a resolute vocation of boxing-onwards. Wolf inspects other people's lives
for schadenfreude. The lily neck of something gentler.
Meekness inheriting meekness. A coward's friendship.
A beast as a placeholder for what is broken.

Textbook

I am soft boiled. A citrus mouldering in the clutch of other fruit.
I am sacrificial, spent slowly on the cake knife that offers me
around a table where everyone wants just a sliver.
There is freedom in deference. The display of small bows.
I rot slow and warm in the clasp of whiteware,
and tin-openers rusted shut. I want to be brave enough to be angry.
I want to bring the house to its knees with a necklace of gasoline,
in a poem with no fire escape. I want to break glass like bread,
and feed it to people too innocent to know better.
I want to outsource the horror-choir that oozes from streetlamps,
and make a papier-mâché of a monster I cannot see.
I will sit on command. Sitting is a thing I do well.
I want to hold you under, the length of time it takes to see the credits
in a revelation of physiology. Is your name where you left it?
In the soap dish on the sink ledge? I have washed and washed
but the song in my head stays the same. La la la la la la la.
I am a veteran chronic. I want to hold anger by the gills
and drown him with air. La la la la la la la la.
Listen, I have spent years riding my skull like a bicycle.
I know what it takes to moulder gently on an ironing board,
or to sun-bleach by a window ledge. I want to rage in a supermarket,
to throw tins of salmon across an aisle for the boldness that entails.
La la la la la la la. I want to rise like the first son, and collapse
rung by rung doing something spectacular. I want to spit
my teeth into a paper bag, and hold a corkscrew to my temple.
I want my monument to whistle, and be torn down
by a more orthodox cognition. I am a sucker, though.
I wear my pathology like a sandwich board.
I wear my sandwich board like shame. Look, I will acquiesce.
La la la la la la. It is all I can do.

Fire

The ferry terns vanish from the pier, a dozen each season.
A headland, gentle as soft-shell crab, loses meat to the tide.
Gorse lights a million candles along the nape of a hill.
Yesterday, a fire alarm mistook smoke for steam.
Today they smelled gas in the playground but found it to be sewage.
And here, the beige livery of a garden left all summer.
And here, rat bait tucked into the elbows of a workshop frame.
Yesterday, they lit a Catherine wheel and couldn't put it out.
We mow where the grass had burned, rake the rotting windfall
from the plums. Today the sky is orange from the bushfires.
Yesterday my uncle said it's a storm in a teacup,
like a teacup has spilled over the Tasman Sea and the fire alarms
are birds, black and wailing, the shrieked bodies of eucalyptus.
I don't know whether Gondwana is fact or a metaphor for poets.
Some days, I feel the universe is a group hug that breaks
into a handshake, and now blows kisses, distanced by fields.
The weatherman says tomorrow is orange, and the next day.
My uncle is a nice man who thinks climate change
is what politicians do when they're bored. Here, the kākā
moves in silence above the cliff, studying its prey for apathy.
The clouds write poems that we take out of context.
Then the kākā will say *fire fire*.

The luck of things

I was tricked to wonder at the god of me.
The pews hold the buttocks of animals too sick and salty
to recognise a miracle when it happens.
The church leaks milk from its udders, and the animals covet it,
limp-footed and blessed by the welcomer who sponges down the altar.
I was duped by a man bleating on a city corner.
I saw him hold to the god, white-knuckled,
and carve up towers like a clove-pocked ham. I saw him nailed
to a power pylon, the asphalt below him made holy
with piss and rubberneckers. I sluiced down a cobbled square.
I don't believe in heaven, but in body fluids of the divine.
In my afterlife I'll be mopped into the recess between the refrigerator
and the wall. I'll be a square of tobacco in the saddlebag of a cowboy
who'll meet the arrowhead before he meets emphysema.
My potency is predicated on a narrowing of disaster. Yeah.
I was tricked to tithe to a hall of dead players. The god trafficked
my remorse to the dark web, where abulia grows slow as teeth.
I pray and pray that I know serenity by the lisping of consonants.
I cannot change the havoc that wreaks out of me. I cannot pray
for a surrogate Gaia. For a motion from train wreck to cot to fleshy egg.
I can pray for the routes forward, for the weavers and cutters
to scythe me a path through the ginger weed and nasturtiums.
I'm unholy and full of the luck of things.

Passengers

An elephant has a trunk, as does a 1980s sedan.
Sometimes a blind man will reach for bitumen.
Sometimes a blind man will reach for leather.
If an elephant has a trunk, it is to drive him
in the direction of plenty – roots, the midges of a water-ditch,
a jackalberry tree, sunlight that holds the wildered frieze
by the scruff of its neck. A car is a thing towards opening.
The back black of unleaded petrol bled into the picnic rug.
Lumber-smell and rubber-smell and spearmints and pool salts.
If I am a hostage in the trunk of things, memory is a night
proximate as smother. What is this black sky?
If you listen hard, you can hear the shape of things to come.
All the tangled plotlines surfacing at one terminal point.
A mobile phone is a thing of pulse. It keeps the heartbeat
between gravel and tarseal. Can you hear *help*
and can you answer to a silence? An elephant is a vehicle
of mass destruction. A hapless thing, blundering –
wrong foot by wrong foot, towards the back of a Toyota Corolla.
He does not mean it. Does he? The car is driving him
in a straight line and he pretends to steer, to four-wheel glide.
The elephant just does as it does, takes the state highway
past industrial rivers and chimneys and cows too tired
to look the glue-house in the eye. I am not a passenger,
but a missionary, driving home *fact* the best way I can.
If he opens the trunk, will the streetlights burn my skin?
Will I forward-roll on to a collision course with wonder?

I am ready for this. I have been waiting all my days.

My final gift

Not the ranch under a   slumping sky, clouds rusted as barns,
the evening turning like a knife. I am not   where you think   I am.
I was never   there,   not with the swell of saddle thrown
to   spooked horses, moon-blind, but knowing the panic
of passivity.   I did not break anyone in, only my second colt, only
my final gift   of a gumline of gravel. Nostrils that   witness their own heat.
Not here: a running iron biting like a coral snake   a running woman
branded by the petroglyphs of someone   too small to stand.
I am tenderfoot in alluvial sand.   I dodge black ice   devil's funnels
every kind of weather.   Not groundwater surfacing.
You will not find me here. I am on a fork in a road,   boxing midges
from my yellow wrists.   Gods shine my shotgun   and
I spit on my boots.   Past the cradle,   past the smoking dogwood
a woman runs to the bottomlands.   My boy
she says   my boy   my boy.

I hope this is mine

In the dream I'd plagiarised a line about despair,
unwittingly. I fell awake, a bonfire with my silly flare
held to the city like the worst firework in the box.
The woman at the superette says I am getting fat.
I apologise when I buy sugar snakes and sherbet;
I say *I'm so sorry* and I eat in cupboards,
not mall food courts or street-side restaurants
where the menus guard the door, bouncers
holding my weekly dole money by the scruff of its neck.
Why are poor people fat? says the lady on television,
stroking the pudge of her Labrador. Irony.
I think that is the start of someone else's story.
I think I am trying to model my opus on Alanis Morissette
now that she's cool again. Like she was cool
in the first place; like the 1990s was a decade made
for whippet children, all grunge and fine bones,
who might shrug at history for a while,
then feed nervous breakdowns, casual as rice.
In the dream I am holding a Labrador
and it is someone else's guide dog but I'm rude
and an antagonist in a story I really wish I'd written.
I fall awake again, and I'm apologising for sugar snakes
and the superette manager smirks and waves me out.
I eat my sugar snakes in a telephone box
and write something confessional on the glass,
something really really TMI, like it was written by someone else –
someone in kindergarten when the world goes up in smoke.
When I fall awake, I'm sobbing down the phoneline
trying to contact a Labrador about some lyrics
I thought were mine.

Stolen pepeha

My mother is the night owl. My father is the tussock.
I own memories, alone. My celestial object is done for.
The rust core of a lamp that was already out – a red star coughing
through light-years of average days, days spent picking lemons
and walking average suburbs, nodding at ordinary dogs.
I know my trespasses by the ghosts of them. I can find the switch, still.
I can hold my hands to the glow of the fire escape,
and watch them burn into yellow petals. Every night,
I weigh my felonies against the basalt clot of heart.
I was young once. I did things. Do you remember who I am?
The forecast was for sleet, the kind that whiplashes your brainstem
and forces birds from their roosts in the dendritic arbour.
I was young and so afraid – escalators and elevators, paddling pools.
When the lamp is out, what do you see? I see me as the river,
marbled with cow scat and duckweed. I see the yawning dark,
the fine down that night makes of all things. This is where I'm going.
There is a mountain where I'm always at the bottom.
I stole the mountain in my sleep. I did things. I held the ignition
until the blue flame slammed into life. My ocean is allegorical.
There are no fish in my stories. The blue flame was never enough
to acquire a heartbeat. I walked here myself. Seventeen, and crashing
into cabinetry like it was my own. My mountain watched me resist,
up every street, through every average day. Do you remember,
I came to keep my nouns in one plastic bag. It was my prerogative,
said the man prescribing my fate. I ate the pills like I wanted to
want to. I watched people talk round corners. I owned everything
in my mind. I was the river. The river was my prerogative.
I was young and full of the soft tongues of milk cows.
I did things, you don't need to know. I was a sorcerer of suburbs

so coiffured that only the moon disrupted the minimalist chic.
I picked lemons, once. I nodded at ordinary dogs.
My retreat was a series of dominoes waiting to fall.
My mountain is the crowd I left there.
Now I am old.

If Vivaldi were under a CTO

Summer

The registrar speaks through us.
The ink the plums make. The sound of sunlight falling
into a wicker trash basket. The world as supple as an unrequited hug.
We buy tinfoil hats like we can live together.
We will live together.
Animals will move in and out of bedrooms.
There are dogs with plums in their hot mouths.
If I had myself by the neck …
If I had myself flat in the face …
There are things I can do that you don't want to know.
If I could be a Spice Girl I would be the lost one.
The girl with the flowers in the trash.
She speaks through us. *God*, you say.
Animals bump against us like they want to say something gratuitous.
You say dogs can't talk. You say he's one son-of-a-bitch you'll never work out.
The bedrooms we spooned in. The plums. The summer we lost our minds.

Autumn

You say that a stitch in time saves nine. Not the tenth. The plums are dead.
This is enough about the moon to know it's disaffected. Yellow bellied, guilt-stars
lead you to outdoor furniture. A sun umbrella slashes your sorrow in halves.
We are two people in a garden, bled out in ochre. We are each other's myth.
Your leaves are coming off. I sweep them into piles that look like hope.
We will burn them later. This is not winter, but this is everything first.

Winter

You drunk-dial your dead friends.
You are one gerund away from defeat.
We know something of sitting on the windowsill
watching the hospital bins clatter below.
The poplar trees are nothing more than electrical cable and water.
It is raw. At this time of year, you can see the skeletons
beyond the brickwork, the ice settling on the windshield,
legs crossed and waiting. You say you can climb a conservatory wall
like you can bark up the wrong plum tree.
This month, the trees all sound the same.
You watch prepositions for intent.
Inside, the nurse is a smile that holds a thimble of dread.
The windowsill needs a lick of paint like you
need a litre of kerosene and a Bic lighter.
You have bad hair. You would be on fire. There is a medicine for that.

Spring

The plum tree is a shock of itself.
We are the stimulants of people who see us in snatches. *Look there.*
You can only touch a green thing with your mind.
If a daffodil hosts somebody lonely and soft,
it is not by intent. What else?
The woman who reads newspapers to the blind,
or the woman who writes poetry in Wingdings,
or the woman who has sex with the bathroom light on,
knows the plum tree from a distance. She keeps a metre
the size of a continent between us. What else?
Everything is exponential. We catch ourselves dancing
on a transformer box, on the outskirts of a neighbourhood.

We might be taken by police, torches down a cul-de-sac,
a gated community where the dogs stand at fence lines, apologetic.
We might be restrained in someone's backyard tennis court,
injected by the unicorn inflatable or the pizza oven.
It's spring and the adults rise like flowers,
at a distance approximating reality television.

The gospel

There is a passage in the Bible somewhere about a lass
knocked up by a prevailing wind. The girl who faked a baby.
The girl who faked cancer. The girl who didn't have anything
to add to a book where the body count rises like a messiah.
There is an argument about God that ends with canned laughter.
There is an argument about God, where God walks off the stage
and into the audience. God turns down a polygraph test.
God refuses to listen to the paternity results, stares down his children
who have the noses of their mothers, the slight cardia
of animals that will never be omnibenevolent, whose love
is milk and bone and fades out like cities on the empire's belt.
The audience cheers when the sign says 'audience cheer'.
The audience sucks their teeth, and holds their breath like fish.
There is a passage in the Bible where everyone in the audience
gets a new Honda. There is a dance track as the host walks in.
The Holy Ghost holds the megaphone and speaks in tongues.
Are you ready? says the invisible, and they pretend he's there.
Are you ready? and a clap spreads through the audience
like venereal disease. A week later, YouTube floods
with God clips. From the crow's nest Noah tweaks the algorithm
to keep the Doomsdayers counting down to the next ep.
There is a passage in the Bible where the show gets cancelled.
There is a passage in the Bible where the Bible is daytime TV reruns,
where the Bible is wedged between one infomercial and the next,
between the Ab Rider Pro and the magnetic underlay,
between the carrot dicer and the stomach-tuck underwear,
between Genesis and a commercial about life insurance.

Vertical

whether we saw the skyline for its dentistry,   or did not.

      whether the sky was bathwater-grey, and we poked it with our small hands.

whether the telephone wires   and mynah birds grew dizzy from their heights.

or the mollyhawk patrolled the alley for yesterday's fish and chips.

I am a person of small intent.   I will follow a landscape to its   third act,

and clap   where the estuary meets the supermarket.   a heron might spook

the trolley bay, regarding my bag of celery with derision.

I might sing a shanty in the megamall, or call   ghosts   from the boat ramp

where the   basalt licks   at the shoreline – dark bodies sprawled

like   cats.   most days, I trudge the beach, like it's the   only   thing   I know.

dogs skitter over the grit, pursuing   whatever dogs pursue.

      a tennis ball, a way of life, office blocks piloted by   little men,

lighthouse keepers who divert   pain   and cost, by a series of spreadsheets.

dogs   do   dog things   and,   whether we know it,

we   do   people things –   folding into escalators, summoning

     empty carparks, leaning against bakery windows

where the scones are warm   and the pies are cold.   whether or not

     it matters.

Visitor

Meet me in the dog-tender night / in the slick of salt grasses and glassworts /
The coagulants of a city struck by tides and trawlers and men in small dinghies /
The houseboats on the mudbanks and the kidney pools, families shifting inside
caravans / Atropos sleeps with her hammer under the mattress / This city is full of
wolves / who know the driveway to her pain / This city is predicated on heat / Every
hillock is waiting to undo itself / to spill its cargo into the sea / Meet me outside the
floodlit embassy / I am sick but I know how to cling / to a softer determinism / The
cul-de-sac unzips like a goddess / Can I speak of consent? / Your hands finger the
fuzz of streetlamps / worry the corners of houses / ease the dogs from their kennels
/ and into a night heaving / with eyelids and rain and stars / The convenience shops
are small beacons / in a slick of cemented trees / alleyways / adult-stores / Atropos'
drunken bile is a tributary / little deus ex machina / the rain is a small intervention
/ holds her hair back while she stoops / Meet me / in the flax-hungry settlements /
in a boarding house where the microwave / is on top of the telly / Meet me in rusted
sinks / and clotheslines that flinch / under the chokehold of a macrocarpa tree / at
the top of a volcano / or at the bottom of a volcano

Amor fati

The mind's crenelations and watchtowers, a moraine of people cast aside
by something so big it might be God. We are armchair surveyors of time,
speculators of drooped intentions that make us feel like we will it so.
We are a half-life of a story about hands that hold tools, beating earth
and its creatures into function. We are scaffolding and cement mixers
and pneumatic drills, pegging time to form. Crows mock us from their grottos,
tap tapping code with their black beaks. They know that will is a crash-dummy
of things that happen, a sacrifice left unacknowledged on the altar,
flyblown and wet. They hold the black of their beaks like candles,
following the blood-scent and the metal of a fate that is cutthroat.
Heavy on the black willow, they banshee-scream and pickaxe
a skyful of animals who can't register the horror.
The fate we must love is a slip-road, lined with the lives
we shed, skins of people we might have been if we'd never blinked
but burned our eyes to cataracts on ecstatic summer.
Crows gather each outer shell and take it up a path we cannot follow.
They say *aye, aye* and chase us onwards, *aye, aye,* and chase us
to a field of unfamiliar trees, again and again. Time meets us there.

Nostalgia is a thing of the past

O brother, this is an ugly way to unlearn hope. How do we forget
stairways and two-car garages and the pillar of imperative that is a woman?
We were kids with birds in our small mouths. We didn't know how to chew.
I summoned you, to be witness to my sorrow. Remember the moon
is upside down here; the man is struggling to reclaim its surfaces.
You are more than a witness to my sorrow. Star-drunk and giddy
and struck by the shoulders of those mesmerised hills, we were right
to believe in magic, the tricks of small animals falling on to empty countertops.
I can bleed rabbits. I can forget this territory of gods who couldn't
give two hoots about the disappearing people. The curtains all fall
in the direction of despair. Yet! O boy, you and I form a lattice of elbows
that only childhood can conjure. Stubbed toes and wobbly fangs
and shin splints that happen when you outgrow yourself, twice over.
Every day the sun gets up is a kind of sleepy magic. Our bunkrooms
hold to ghosts even when we lose the power to believe.
O brother, you are the trick of the light, the balloon quadrupeds
and everything that I could hold up my sleeve. We are the photographs
and we are the quiver of cells that keep walking on and on,
sometimes without us. If you are a witness, you are the wizard
whose alchemy is to hold us here, upright, and grinning.
We knew the man in the moon couldn't handle us. Yet!
We were birds in the mouths of gods who don't give two hoots.
O brother, we made our own cause. We danced.
We danced like disappearing people.

Immunohistochemistry

We pipette soluble proteins like mothers do. Mothers are no minor characters,
who arrange herbs like rubrics, under the soft light of a kettle stove.
Home is a fume-cupboard where legend is filtered like breath.
Our mothers huddle around pantries of cod liver oils, vitamins, and bleach.
Their hands haul the sun over the eastern hillocks, like an axiom.
We know them by induction – every morning opens, a promise
to people we haven't met before, to a clusterfuck of mass and motion.
We stain the antibodies with the colours we would wear if we were brave.
Our mothers move the embers in the stove. The herbs are too dead.
Little glow that cannot meet our gummy eyes – a flintwheel
in a forest of people who worship rubble like it is celestial,
and the celestial like it is God. We stain the god like it is someone to hold to,
something that sticks when the antigens creep up our stairwells,
and take the last good thing we have. Our mothers. Our dim, perfect animals –
beasts that pin us to our words. Beasts that hurt more than a blood tie ever will.
We are the blotted ghosts, dark oblongs on the metaphysical pastes
that glue our stories to the fabric of family.
We should all go out together, little glow of inadequacy,
when the sun plays truant and the mothers pick mint from a garden
struck still by grief. We would hold our best mammals
under a streetlamp that erases us.
We would hide, from gods and scientists, in light.

Relatives

I like to have reunions with the people we used to be
when we were better people. I like to pull the gear shaft into reverse,
and hope for a past that runs smooth and slow.
My future is heatwaves and nectarines, the assertion of a waterline
on the plimsoll of a container ship. I like to think I am the kind of person
who shrugs off a retirement fund, who jogs on the spot
at seventeen, twenty-seven, and forty-two, chasing a dream
Einstein had – something about ping pong on a train
and the lonely man on the platform, watching watching.
I was real once. I was an artefact of my ancestors' retching –
ambergris heaved up on to a reef, wrecked and waiting
to prove my worth in salt. I practise being alone,
so that when I die solo on a gurney I won't need cue cards
to tell myself I'm not okay. I guess you might call it self-compassion.
I like to breathe into a paper bag, and be happy.
I am happy relative to the woman with a trundler of celery.
I am happy relative to the peristaltic gut of a sperm whale.
I am happy relative to Buridan's ass and two bales of hay.
I like to imagine I'm the type who has inimitable swagger;
that my kid-self would regard me with feverish hands;
that all the heatwaves and nectarines in a summer haze
might make an emperor of me. I used to like who I was.
I used to imagine my swagger would take me places –
over the phoenix palms and Norfolk pines, to a present
where I could tally up redeeming qualities, and yowl my name,
and take selfies – like – there's me taller than a Scottish terrier,
or there's me faster than a roadside Zimmer frame,
or there's me watching a beam of light like
I'm the loneliest person in the world.

Time

If time is a ladder. If time is a diving platform. If time is brushstrokes
on a shifting canvas. If time is the dog tethered to the clothesline.
If time is everything, exactly where they left it. A glove on an upturned hoe,
or all the poems caught mid-howl to the moon. If time is a septic tank.
If time is a gully of nasturtiums, a bucket of mustard flowers,
or a clocktower's hands clambering noonwards. If time is aspirational.
I hold your cold-blooded asymmetry in my head. I take the train twelve stations,
to a stop where the houses are small and square. If time is a ticket warden.
If time is the rust-metal and scoria, the slur of graffiti along a defunct tunnel.
If time is the tunnel, loping from one suburb to the next. A light.
The pylons hold the body of the thief above his people. Sheep don't look up,
can't fathom a world beyond the hay and sod. The people rinse their crockpots,
and pray and shit, as though the holy spirit is a single mum
who puts Fanta in the lunchboxes, but loves her children
more than a heaven ever could. If time is pins and needles on a school mat.
If time walks on water but doesn't know how to swim.
If time is body-shamed at the public pools, or too deep too fast.
If time is a game of rock-paper-scissors on a chlorine bleacher.
The dairy owner sells mixed candy to the Iscariot lad, at three dollars a bag.
The sherbet coins taste like nostalgia, but also more like guilt.
If time is what holds talent to the cross. If time makes traitors out of love,
and rides shotgun and wild from a liquor store ramraid.
If time holds you under water until you are a real brother.
If time wears a balaclava or a uniform. If time makes liars out of us all.
The single mum waits at the station
for her child to arrive, backpack slumped over one shoulder.
We are all carrying things we cannot bear.
Time makes an ashtray of the evening.
Time multiplies the barks of dogs along the valley road,
to where the berms are overgrown, the apple trees untouched.

Naming the beasts

The planes went down the same day Romulus and Remus
were butchered. Winter –
and I walked barefoot through the cattlegrass,
mooed to Romulus and Remus
and they said *how do you do?*
as though it were an ordinary Tuesday.
As though the stock truck
parked outside the old schoolhouse
were just a metaphor for everything
thrust into double digits. The sky was cheesecake.
Sweetgums were bald to skin and bone. Wind licked
the bluegrass, retelling comedies
only the weather sees. What world is this?
Romulus and Remus were the hot breath
rising from the schoolhouse kettle,
the two sparrows that knocked against the car windshield
on that lonely highway. They were a pair of headlights.
They were possums spent on nightfall, giddy
with the casual light of passing tankers.
Romulus and Remus loped on to the truck ramp,
said *how do you do?* And I. And I. And I.
I walked barefoot through embers only to turn back halfway,
to shrug at the ordinary Tuesday, to let what happens
happen. I hid from the bellowing, under husk and chaff,
in the noise of harrower and winnower.
Later, I sat in the diner, watched two planes go down on a city,
into the stubble of people and places
just doing what people and places do.
As though little men falling from windows
were just a metaphor for everything haunted
by what we never fix.

It will blow over

The storm-birds sing of an underworld, strangle-held by retaining walls
and purpling weeds. They fluster the sky, circle the vacant fields
like bodyguards, bother the cattle, spit shadows over the day grasses.
The clouds are dragged behind the wheels of an SUV.
The clouds are the shape of victims. A time-lapse of shame,
one milky figure mounting another, like that's all there is.

The storm is another lifetime that passes us by. A predation
founded on counterfactuals. Above the clocktower, a lightning rod
heckles the destroyer. Time holds its breath between brackets,
chews the borage flowers and smooths the minds of slow animals.
It will not condemn the enemy. It will not metabolise a slur,
cussing the metaphysical from a place of routine grief.

The storm-birds know me for my ordinariness. My blunt skull.
I am a creature who resists chemistry. Punchlines skitter
from my surfaces. My rage is elemental but moves as slow as guilt.
I appropriate the sunny side of humans who have better things to do.
I take Love and run for the hills,
to bury it someplace iced-over and immortal.

The storm-birds move through me like I'm a haunted house.
I shudder myself awake. I shake the ghosts from the insulation fibre.
I spook the swallows from the chimney pot. I am the red zone
of a Beaufort scale. If I crouch in the crawlspace, it is not for life,
but for beauty – the collision of things on a metal road at night.
The gentle turning of a headlight towards the moon,

the blush of the dead-end's fugitives. The storm that moved over us
like a miracle. Or the storm that moved us like a miracle.
The storm-birds cannot tell the difference.

God of nations

There are detours through this kingdom I didn't know.

There are summer horses and stone fruit that cap the hills.

The snouts of earthmovers, excavating dread.

Every drought starts off egalitarian and moves into something picky.

The scruples of a pampas flower, the skink who moves in and out of moonlight.

There is a heat that stills our thirst. There is thunder-clapped dune,

and the caves we could not hunch in for the myths they shelter.

This is a dream sequence that takes me from the Bombay Hills

to the flatlands of cruel mathematics. This is a dream sequence

where I can love you and hold a bayonet at the same time.

This is not a desert but regret. This is not heat but absence.

This is a dream sequence where you run naked from the boot of a sedan.

This is a dream sequence where a hundred barn owls watch you run.

I didn't know there was a shortcut, through the house on fire,

and past the smelter and between turbines that cut the ghosts into ribbons.

I want to say I know this place with my eyes closed.

I can run, butt naked, through cabbage rows and dairy cows,

and the Waikato will annunciate my name with a branding iron

and an ear tag that speaks to a bloodline sniffed out by regret.

I am writing in my first language. My second is shame.

When I dream I dream in words I cannot spell.

Mapping old stars

Witness this: the kid skitters dog-wild, her bucket knocks her knees.
The man is a man and not a wolf. He howls summer, all evening,
when the sky is hot and star-heavy, and his tobacco tastes like the edge
of a field where he watched cricketers move slow as grass.
The kid is a thing that moves without willing. The man smells of memory.
The man is a man and the kid is a kid. The man will drag his tail
through low-lit avenues, remarking on the furniture of better homes,
televisions seizing in the corners of living rooms.
The kid will sniff the transformer box for stories. The kid will tell tales
to mosquitoes, summoning a gallery of whispers in January's cul-de-sac.
The man will tug the leash, like he owns the route
home, like the night is for arrival. The doormat says something in Latin.
Est modus in rebus. What can that mean, but the little gooseberry lanterns
and the sage plant and the thistle, all sit about waiting for purpose?
There is measure in a tic that worries the flesh, as there is measure
in the reddening lamp of a star named after its keeper.
The kid wraps her dog-tongue around nouns pulled light-years backward.
If she lets go – will everything spring forward and all at once?
Four forces study her from the quealed garden –
father, mother, brother, sister. There is measure in each.
She sits on the shoulders of a man who knows the darkness by its takings.
The summer is a memory of a memory, an anachronistic flare
that defies a history of diminishing returns.

Hard sell

There is a robot in this poem,
because I want it, and you get what you want
when you call the shots in a poem.
I am a victim in this poem because I choose to be.
This is not free will. This is choosing to put pineapple on pizza,
not because it's good, but because it's necessary.
I walk the talk and sometimes I worship dogs,
like their agenda is telic. Like they are pulling me in the direction
of finish lines, where all things are greeted by ticker tape
and water. The robot in this poem doesn't want to be here.

There are two people with empty speech bubbles
looking down the barrel of a telephone jack.
And I might be at one side of a limerick about a man from Huntly.
And you might be on top of a senryū peering down on commercial bins
and people who carry themselves like nits, scuttling in and out
of storefronts. The robot is still here.

Soft determinism puts pineapple on my pizza,
and I want to want to agree that fruit and saccharomyces
are the Bonnie and Clyde of unsuspecting kitchens.
The robot does what he's told, but doesn't want to
know the results of his Turing test. God!
the pineapple is something that you can take or leave,
and you will, you will.

I'm doomed to put pineapple on pizzas.
I might be the theandry of parts and pieces,
predicated on a harder problem that catches itself in snatches.
I might drop something about objective collapses
because I know more about poetry than physics
but want you to register the reverse.
I want to wear my limited knowledge of quantum superposition
and radioactive decay on my t-shirt,
like I could be a cool cat, or not.

If I were a robot, I would be in a better poem.
If I were a person, I'd want the telephone wires to hum like stars,
and the stars to be unavoidable.

What we wish

Little brain, small trail where breadcrumbs lead to ovens.
I am here with a pocket of twigs and slight wishes.
Velleity is what I wanted to say, if you understood
what it meant to live in pieces, to want as discretely as a bobby calf.
I have unseen the eyes of a mother roll upwards and white,
where her child is hauled into the backseat of a wagon.
I have unseen the good dog volunteering his animal
to a person who wants violently and fast. *Velleity*
is how I keep myself small. My little brain, waiting
with a basketful of berries, at the door of a gingerbread flat.
Little brain saying *knock knock* so soft nobody knew
the etiquette of answering. I have unseen the fire climbing
the cladding. I have unheard a misery of stars burned to the filter.
I'm a slosh of cerebral spinal fluid, and places where trees
root down. I'm a hunter's scent at the carfax
where other people's stories start in a gesture so arbitrary
it is consigned to doom. Little brain, we go left or right
but always home. Our wishes catch on the soft hairs
of fate – a trail set, a fuse lit, a gentle zigzag held to sentence.

Road trip with my adolescent self

You say *what is the point?*
If a tree falls in Alice Springs, does it make a sound?
The cattle truck rattles past our '89 Holden.
Finches rise from the saltbushes. The day is a kiln-fire,
the soil – seven years sober and bone dry.
Knock knock you say, and I say *who's there?*
like you didn't see the dingo and the death adder;
you don't see the glut of rust and zinc,
the bloodwood lifting dumbbells above the steeple
of the burnt-out gum, the sky dumb and blue
as the Cookie Monster. *What is the point?* –
like you don't see powerlines and powerlines,
hooves that storm the dead and the forgotten, lightning that licks
along the orange hillocks. You don't see what I see.
I need you to see what I see. You are fifteen
and the desert can only be a metaphor for absence.
Absence is a witchery, stark as a Baptist church
hunching in the wilderness. Everything is hot and waiting
to ambush you from the sedges. *Knock knock.*
If a tree falls in Alice Springs, it weeps like a lost child –
who doesn't know where to turn when the starting-gun fires.
Who's there? Only the timeworn and the spent can hear them.

Cowboys are an animal left too long

The teabag left too long in the sky, steeping   red.   The hackberry struck
by headlights,   wild   and afraid,   cuffed   by the end of another day.
          I used to have a name here.   I arrived in dreams, running, like you,
past the smoked-out manger, through a brushfire where even the birds are lit.
Marsh rabbits and wood rats shiver in the ash-cut stiltgrasses.
          We were animals,   once.   Venom and teeth and mandibles,
all set forward and hungry. You licked all surfaces,   tonguing
the bark splinters and the hot tars. I fed the deer and the old milk cow.
And you   sharpened a picture of a state   down South,
where the wasps knit a paper nest called Confederacy,
          where   names are just things to be taken to the storm drain and
drowned—   Kittens, lapping the gun-powder off your palms.

I remember watching cowboys on a Sunday afternoon,
from a couch at the   bottom of the world.
Popcorn and kettle chips,   a teabag left   too long in the mug.
You used to have a name here.   We ran   through the cabbage trees,
past the pylons, all humming with   dreams.
Brown sheep white sheep black sheep.   We walked the suburbs
and wondered if we'd see spurs or a holster like you see in the   real   outback
          in a shopping mall in a stadium in a mosque.   It felt so far away.
Men walking through the saloon doors   with a gun.
          We used to play it in the yard with the sprinklers and the dog.
Did you see him? we'd say, yap yapping and   shooting our finger pistols.
          Did you see this happening? we'd say later.   *Did you?*

The toll

A poem is a road of bitumen and sorrow,
between two places we never agreed to like.
You flatten my name, a window closing on a bird-neck,
a window eyeballing an internal wall for its television.
My bird-neck was founded on knots – anchor hitch and butcher's knot
hunter's bend and soft shackle. If I wanted to wend the road
between my place and yours, I would pay the toll of us.
I would drive under the bridge. And, maybe, I would stand over the bridge
and drop a boulder like it was just a moment where history hit and ran.
The judge would say my name and I would close against a court
that knows a poem is just a poem, not a route out.
This is a myth – a penny thrown from the Empire State Building
will kill a person on the street below. This is a myth – an overbridge
is the only poem I know, the only way I see the milestone-tree
that holds the world steady like an eyelash. I am in stitches.
I am a window closing on a sea of branches. I am gesture
that is burning to its filter. I am the last time I saw myself
as a person, chewing gum at a carfax – a decision-maker, a bird.
The knot holds me like I am a landscape of bulk, one bird-neck
upon another in a painting where everything is sky.
A poem is just what we say when we are concentrating on the road;
what we never say. The toll is what we carry from space to space.

We go down together

We have no names for our ancestors –
not for the one wading through a swarf of wheat,
the sun sticking to the drystone walls,
not for those ones idling in the alleyways,
or passing the windfall of a summer plum.
We have no words for the one with the machete,
sat fever-trembling in the Sumerian paradise
with carnelian pears and cattle shit and willpower
that looks back twice before walking into the lake.
We all have stones in our pockets.
There are no sounds where we lower ourselves
into the foisty mines of our grandparents.
There are no sounds where we blind ourselves
to the words text provokes, where we know
the paths of buzzards but can't break
the grapheme's hex. We have forgotten kith
and the torched hills, the witchery of gardens –
barrenwort and bloodroot that only a woman
could love. Our encyclopedias cannot speak
to the glisk of the campfire, the queer smell of kerosene
on the skin of one who burned a whole forest
to carry us. You and I take the stones
from our pockets, and throw them into the clough –
Scrabble tiles spelling invalid words;

animals;   exiles.

I forgot why I came

Every soft hunger, dispossession of a muscle memory,
the ginger root and the mozzies here to plagiarise a song.
Every short chord, the sparklers that spell cuss words,
and we danced the mozzies to their deaths. Sing!
I am home enough to know the wolf in the wallpaper.
Every tea towel holds a scent of somebody's Yesterday.
I can't remember if I said *open sesame* or just entered.
Sing! Streetlamp rattled with the memory of a younger filament.
Sing! Sorry takeout sign that blinked like another neon
on a night that made more impression. I have failed.
The jigsaw was a thousand pieces, and all of them salt-blue.
The sky is another thing I can't complete. Look,
I came to this weather with a plan to pray, sing,
venerating a sisterhood of neglect. I walk and watch my feet
like they might remind me how Time dodges all the marshals
and cones and starting-guns, and puts me here.
Here. Every soft motion, every slip of the tongue,
moves me a little further from your door. I am home enough
to watch the wall clock gesture hours I wouldn't dare.
I can't remember if I told you this before. I like to dance –
I am home enough to dance the way I remember.
Somebody told me Yesterday knew me inside out.
The jigsaw consummated, the sparklers burned to the wire.

When I try to meditate the waterbuck explodes

Bam! There's a stampede of waterbuck inside me.
Bladder-hoof and gut-bleat. My heartbeat keeps pace
as they skip river and ravine, chasing the southerly down-coast
to where I sit in my stupor; where mosquitoes
swill around the ceiling fan. I am an animal bomb.
I'm photo-bombing a family selfie where everybody looks sad.
Look at me! I'm a runner and a ruminant; dogfood and prey.
Bam! Just yesterday I put a dinner knife in an electric toaster.
Bam! Just yesterday I chased my tail around the laundry room.
Bam! Just yesterday I snorted ten grams of pool cleaner
and lay on a floatation device, my waterbuck bones rocking.
Sometimes I set off the alarms at airport security;
I catch in the turnstile outside Parliament. Customs spray DDT
into my hot mane, while the sniffer dogs slink into corners.
I'm trying to think about thinking about absence.
I'm doing a full-body scan from frown to squat,
but I'm a ticking IED. I'm brindled and bearded and hell-bent
on celebrity. I'm a full-page spread. *Look!* I'm giddy as a starlet.
My waterbuck gums grin fatuous as doom.
Years after I explode, they'll be wiping the toothpicks
and the hobnails from their faces. *Bam!*
I'll be a small speed bump in the karma of other species;
a transcendental plague. I'll be the vexation that belies Zero,
the final collapse of the yogic beast.

The penultimate garden

Boy, this is my whimpering kingdom. This is my heirloom defeat
muzzling the potato shaw. This is the salt words on our lips,
the nasal bark the oxen make, swaying in an open field.
This is neonicotinoids souping in a paddock. This is the last bees
on the clovergrass. Our final smokestack fingering the sky
like it is more than a lid on a snagged animal.
Boy, if I said I am shy, would you buy it? A small snail,
me, shrinking to the touch. If every neckbone flutters
to the beating of the loader, if every heart beats to the excavator's
heavy head, would you believe I am so lonely
I could have them dig a hole for me to crouch?
Boy, this is my penultimate garden. Here the marrow turn and turn
over soft soil. Here the broad beans spill over each other
like drunken goons. I have pricked out an entire punnet
of things that live even when they have forgotten why.

You will know what to do with them.

Breaking news

There is another mass shooting. The pangolin curls into a tenpin ball,
and we are iodine in the veterinarian's cubby hole. We are swabs and cotton
and all the ways we could have been gentler. The world is a baby. The world is on fire.
The world is a wet market where everybody is smaller than on the packet.
On the packet is a picture of a family of seventeen in the back of a lorry.
Opening the hatch feels uncertain as physics. The world is on fire –
I already said that. The baby is learning grammar. We sway like animals do,
jams in the face of our science. Our knees shake all the way from home
to the pastel colours of harder rooms. They say why don't you lie down.
We are likeable enough. The pangolin is a metaphor for the embarrassment
that lowers itself in waves upon the fire. We have been here before.
I am trying to write about something as real as *Dr. Phil*. I have been banished
time and time again, to a party where everybody has come down with something
beautiful. In the collection tank the rain makes the noise of an animal choking.
They say it's nerves. I don't want to go to Seattle. I don't want to play tenpin
bowling with a visitor who thinks it's cute. We try to be polite in the way Diana
was polite and died in a tunnel somewhere between two places I forget.
The baby has an ontology the size of a pangolin. I visit the wet markets
to remember why I never come here.

Patmos

Even so, Amen.

These are the end words. An equity that shucks all the beasts from their burrows.
A hounding of dreamers.

Sleet that settles on coroner and clay, a green lamp known in sleep.
Ceaseless peristalsis of persons intent on exit strategies.

Every evening sets the bricks on fire, extinguishing the stealth of web and spider.
A god erases its fingerprints.

John is just another man. John is a raffle ticket lost to the burial ground.
Soft breath of wattle, alder, ash. John is nothing special.

If the director is offstage, prompters find their own offerings.
Lines met in darkness, which fall like sleet. John is literate in conclusion.

I don't care to revisit that shrine. This Patmos is not the actual Patmos.
I move through the avenues at night, to my station at the crossroads.

The truck is parked up in mulch of a city intent on unhousing its slag,
of reincarnating offcuts and VCR shards as mosaic. Art.

I am a last theologian, scrutinising a line that walked me here.
John drinks tea in the hallway like he is a line break in a poem about time.

There is a god in the gunfire, a god that moves like a placeholder
for something better. How did it come to this? God.

Where the line enters the sky, I summon
the yardarm, the staircase, the coat stand, the gallows tree.

John tells me not to be so dramatic. He is writing an exegesis
about something small like love. There is no sleet in Patmos, and no junk

offerings to a god who can't find the paperwork to leave a place
where he is landlord to geezers lost to despair. And the wattle pollens – alder, ash,

stick to his god-shoes, clog his god-pipes. John is only one revelation
in a series, a faint artist making gifts from the gaps between prayers.

Fire in the slaughterhouse

Udder milk and cow eyes cataract in the sweltry of time.
All the things I mean to take. The things that hold me under.
I made an escape hatch with my nouns, held the matchstick to my tonsils.
Look. The world is cheap cladding and bedrock.
My rubber hands calculate small things; a cradle full of ants,
stars I have no names for. I want to say I saved my dog first,
not the dog bowl, the ornament, or the book on dogs like my dog,
only fixed and sitting even when the bannister licks orange.
Good dogs, like my dog, inlapidated by time and order.
Witness this hot manger, where I came to the platitudes of wise men.
Fire, motioning between one mammal and the next,
repurposing tangerine into a primary colour. Gas blue.
I want to say I erupted the neighbourhood. I howled
like the dogs in the book don't howl. I saved the best things,
and lined them up along the driveway, waiting for them to spark joy.
A henge of commercial lithics rubberneck. The stars.
A parsimony of fire, no palimpsest of the prime mover,
no fingerprints bound to the fuel or the foible that spoke original sin.
This dog is the real dog. If my work was arson, it was not my intent.
I made the flame weep along the fuse line, but tenderly until fire
mooed the cows, caught in the black throat of the slaughterhouse magpie.
Us beasts, reduced to salts that spasm in the updrafts. Still,
if my work was to shuck the animals from their essences,
to sweep the soft ash of ideas from the sawdust floors,
I would take the things that hold me under. Us desolate souls.
Still. Small as we are.

Dream-deer attends the collapse

Time abandons us in the crook of pine.
A deer wonders why I make sounds with my hands.
If I had a copper coin for every time they thought I'd rise.
If I had knees that could take the upswing, an eyeball that could outstare hope.
The pines are not from here, in the same way I am an adoptee to fate.
We have deep taproots but nothing much else to hold us. Down!
Our little feet wrap around the heart of something that looks like home.
The condo collapsed and all they could see were bunk beds and stars.
My roots make me a victim to damp, to the wet breath that haunts a boy
whose survival insists on one mooring. One slip is a coupling of days
into a single point. The deer is in the crosshairs of my silly pistol.
I am in the crosshairs, in a frame that looks like home. Two windows,
a door, and a chimney to burn all the maps that found me here. Down!
If I had a singlet that spoke my disease. If they shifted the ribbon
at the finishing line, a little closer to my comforts.
If my bootstraps hauled me to surface like a bad carrot –
a deer might wonder why a boy would dream a forest, after all.
What is a boy doing face-down in a sluiceway, his sisters pulling back
stones to see where the scrub and stem begin? This cradle of sugar pine.
This crossbeam, a witness to wanhope. A deer might wonder,
is the boy alone?

And I am a single point where my grandparents,
and their grandparents, made a knot in the earth and held.

Gestalt

Everything here is mountain. The girl yaps inside thistled fields.
Backcountry crags and a dog in auto-focus, and the girl looks up
at a buzzard circling the corrie and its dead animals. *Dog*
the girl says, and the dog jogs outside the panorama.
What if the girl herself were a mountain? Instead, she holds herself
like a small box in somebody else's dream.
She is the drapery behind things. She is the ground cover,
not the poplar tree, the demersal silt beneath the sunken kingdom.
When the girl drinks dandelion hooch she is a ghost named *Here*.
I am here, she says, and the furnaces from Wolverhampton to Smethwick
gutter and strobe. All the dogs in Birmingham bleat, and the pit shafts
in the Black Country shudder as though the earth coughs up a hairball.
The girl is a ghost as faded as distant battleships. The girl is relief –
the gridwork of a spreadsheet, grout between brickwork,
pulp that hugs to text. Here is the girl. Split lip and nosebleed,
shaking a piggybank of hurt like someone might get it.
If someone gets it, the dog will yap inside thistled fields.
The mountains will quiver. There will be no drapery,
no softening frigate. Everything here is the girl.

Drift

Fortune favours the brief. For instance, this crèche of stars bursting in and out of recess.
This sun, half-spent and memorising surfaces, every rock trying for a circle
but drunk and leaning into doorways. Planck time doing rails
off a kitchen countertop. A jar of chutney chasing thermodynamics up a one-way street.
The weak will inherit the earth. A roadside loquat, deferential and misplaced.
A dog's lean mind sharpened on a branch that points to a theoretical heaven.
The clouds bursting like fungi, like cauliflower,
to briefly establish all the ruins of a face. I will grow into it.
I will counter the entirety of a milky way with one snort. I will be a moment held
by the mandibles of something bigger than a god. All bark and no blight.
I will run through the clouds and they will ribbon in the wake of me.
I will be received by a wolf at the door. Anubis will weigh my heart as if I had one.
The poem will be short. For instance: these birds that pour from the hillside;
the cortex embalmed with the data of a forestry; tidelines that force mockery
into mandalas that evaporate with the wind.
Anubis holds our hands to the sternum of a pulsing sky.
This is not our fault. We were carried here like spores. Like spores we open and lie.
Open and lie.

Acknowledgements

Some of these poems have been previously published in *Kissing Dynamite*, *Poetry New Zealand Yearbook 2020, 2021, 2022, Rattle*, and *Kissing a Ghost – New Zealand Poetry Society 2021 anthology*.

This book would be less beastly without the flanking of some exceptional humans. My thanks to the good folks at Otago University Press, including poet and publisher Sue Wootton, Meg Hamilton, Laura Hewson, Mel Stevens and Fiona Moffat. Thanks to Anna Hodge, who with eagle eyes, good humour, and patience, nudged my dodgier spellings and wayward hyphens into shape. Thanks to David Eggleton for shortlisting a version of this collection for the 2021 Kathleen Grattan Award.

Thank you to the mob of humans who keep my noggin in check, to the pubs that fetch me beer and coasters, to the coffee shops that keep me in constant oscillation. *Thank you* to Sly, Chris, Trev, and Julian for being my sunshine. *Thanks* to David Bowie and to my faltering hippocampi. *Thanks* to Anna, Soni, Mel, Uji, Judith and Robert for warmth and comradery on this strange orb. *Thanks* to the medicators, the healers, the respite-givers, and the listeners. Caroline, Shirley, Saffron … *Thank you* to strange cul-de-sacs and to my dog. *Thank you* to daytime talk-shows and spaghetti westerns, to Kim Hill and the ocean. *Thanks* to my family, who suffer the spam of my first drafts. I love you so much! *Thank you* to the Glasgow University gang for contending with my dressing-gown and wild hair and sherry at 3am. *Thank you* to microglia and to the lush lexicon of Robert Macfarlane. And *thanks* to the talented sapiens, who inspire me, and put me off writing ever again, in equal measure, including: Aimée Keeble, Eileen Merriman, Leanne Radojkovich, TS Eliot, Rosetta Allan, Ocean Vuong, Carolyn Gillum, Syd Barrett, Catherine Chidgey, Patti Smith, Tracey Slaughter, Kae Tempest, Siobhan Harvey, Cormac McCarthy, Johanna Emeney, Jack Ross, Alt-J, Bronwyn Lloyd, Michael Steven, Wes Lee … and so many others. This work would be a shell without its mollusc, if not for you.

Published by Otago University Press
Te Whare Tā o Te Wānanga o Ōtakou
533 Castle Street
Dunedin, New Zealand
university.press@otago.ac.nz
www.otago.ac.nz/press

First published 2022
Copyright © Elizabeth Morton
The moral rights of the author have been asserted.

ISBN 978-1-99-004838-8 (print)

Published with the assistance of Creative New Zealand

Editor: Anna Hodge
Cover image: Vecteezy
Author photograph: Richard Doran

Printed in Aotearoa New Zealand by Ligare